HEALTHY® CHOICE

CONDENSED SOUP

RECIPE CREATIONS™

PUBLICATIONS INTERNATIONAL, LTD.

Photography: Sanders Studios, Inc., Chicago

Pictured on the front cover: Mediterranean Chicken *(page 64)*.

Pictured on the back cover *(top to bottom):* Fiesta Chicken with Garlic Sour Cream Sauce *(page 74)*, Penne Pasta Salad *(page 32)*, Bay Village Shrimp *(page 76)* and Artichoke-Pepper Torte *(page 10)*.

ISBN: 0-7853-2282-5

Manufactured in U.S.A.

8 7 6 5 4 3 2 1

Microwave Cooking: Microwave ovens vary in wattage. The microwave cooking times given in this publication are approximate. Use the cooking times as guidelines and check for doneness before adding more time. Consult manufacturer's instructions for suitable microwave-safe cooking dishes.

Creative Ideas from Healthy Choice®

The secret for making delicious, creative recipes for today's tastes!^{SM}

Who has the Time? Today's family is active and always on-the-go. Who has the time to prepare great-tasting, creative and nutritious meals when there are business meetings, soccer games, carpools...

We've got the Answer... At Healthy Choice, we are committed to providing delicious, healthful foods that fit your lifestyle. That's why we've created Healthy Choice® Recipe Creations™, a flavorful and creative line of condensed soups that offer innovative ways to prepare great-tasting recipes.

Distinctive Flavors for Contemporary Cooking... Our delicious flavors each have their own perfect blend of fresh herbs and flavorful spices to add a special touch to your own recipes or that extra something to make quick recipes into great-tasting meals.

Tap into your Creativity... Whether you are an experienced chef short on time or just looking for innovative menu ideas, Recipe Creations™ soups are creative and healthful recipe ingredients to make your meals even more special.

Contemporary Recipe Ideas... From our kitchens at Healthy Choice to yours, we have created great-tasting recipes for all occasions with only the freshest ingredients in mind. The chefs in our kitchen know how special meal time is, so they devised contemporary recipes for today's tastes to provide the perfect healthful dish for every occasion. So whether you are entertaining for brunch, need a creative appetizer to pass, are hungry for a wholesome family meal or just prefer a light salad or sandwich, these recipes offer a wide assortment of enticing and delicious menu ideas.

Know your Nutrition... Because healthful eating is so important, we want you to know how nutritious each recipe is. Following each recipe we have included a Nutritional Analysis that provides the calories, protein and fat grams, percentage of calories from fat and sodium level for each serving. Each serving of Healthy Choice® Recipe Creations™ condensed soup has less than 480 mg of sodium and less than 3 grams of fat. Recipes made with Healthy Choice® Recipe Creations™ have less than 600 mg of sodium and less than 30% of calories from fat to provide excellent nutrition as well as great taste.

EAT what you LIKE™... At Healthy Choice, we make meals better tasting and more nutritious. So people can enjoy eating what they like—and feel good about it. This commitment is the soul of Healthy Choice. As your needs change, we will continue to offer a variety of great-tasting foods incorporating the latest advancements in nutritional learning.

That's why with Healthy Choice® Recipe Creations™ Condensed Soups, you really can EAT what you LIKE.

EAT *what* you LIKE™   HEALTHY CHOICE®

New Beginnings

CRAB TOASTS

1 can Healthy Choice® Recipe Creations™ Cream of
   Celery with Sautéed Onion & Garlic
   Condensed Soup
12 ounces crabmeat or surimi seafood, flaked
¼ cup *each* chopped celery and sliced green onions
1 tablespoon lemon juice
½ teaspoon salt (optional)
⅛ teaspoon grated lemon peel
1 French bread baguette
⅓ cup fat free shredded Parmesan cheese
   Paprika

In medium bowl, combine soup, crabmeat, celery, onions, lemon
juice, salt and lemon peel; mix well. Cut baguette diagonally into
½-inch slices; arrange slices on 2 cookie sheets. Broil 5 inches from
heat 2 minutes until toasted, turning once.

Spread 1 tablespoon crab mixture on each baguette slice. Top with
Parmesan cheese; sprinkle with paprika. Broil 5 inches from heat 2
minutes or until lightly browned. *Makes about 30 appetizers*

NUTRITIONAL ANALYSIS

Per serving:

Calories	50	% Calories from fat	15%
Protein	3g	Sodium	220mg
Fat	1g		

ARTICHOKE–PEPPER TORTE

$2\frac{1}{2}$ cups chopped water bagels (about 3 bagels)
2 tablespoons olive oil
3 teaspoons dried chives, divided
Vegetable cooking spray
2 (8-ounce) packages fat free cream cheese,
    softened
1 (15-ounce) container fat free ricotta cheese
1 can Healthy Choice® Recipe Creations™ Cream of
    Broccoli with Cheddar and Onion Condensed
    Soup
1 (4-ounce) container fat free egg substitute
    (equivalent to 2 eggs)
1 tablespoon salt free ground herbs and spices
1 teaspoon garlic salt
1 (8.5-ounce) can artichoke hearts, drained and
    chopped
1 (15-ounce) jar roasted red bell peppers, drained
    and chopped
1 cup chopped fresh basil

In medium bowl, combine bagels, oil and 1 teaspoon chives; mix well. Spray $9\times2\frac{1}{2}$-inch springform baking pan with vegetable cooking spray. Press bagel mixture into bottom of springform pan. Bake at 375°F 15 minutes; cool.

With electric mixer, combine cheeses, soup, egg substitute, herbs, garlic salt and remaining 2 teaspoons chives; mix well. Spread half the cheese mixture over bagel crust. Top with artichokes and half each of peppers and basil. Spread remaining cheese filling over basil; top with remaining peppers. Bake at 375°F 1 hour or until set in middle; cool. Refrigerate 6 to 8 hours or overnight. Run knife around edge of torte; remove side of pan. Top with remaining basil. Slice thinly and serve with crackers. *Makes 20 servings*

NUTRITIONAL ANALYSIS

Per serving:

Calories	100	% Calories from fat	17%
Protein	8g	Sodium	470mg
Fat	2g		

Artichoke-Pepper Torte

ARTICHOKE DIP

1 (14-ounce) can non-marinated artichoke hearts, chopped
1 can Healthy Choice® Recipe Creations™ Cream of Roasted Garlic Condensed Soup
1 cup fat free cream cheese
½ cup *each* fat free shredded Parmesan cheese, Healthy Choice® Fat Free Shredded Mozzarella Cheese, sliced green onions and roasted red bell peppers
¼ teaspoon black pepper
⅛ teaspoon crushed red pepper (optional)
Salt (optional)
Vegetable cooking spray

In medium bowl, combine artichoke hearts, soup, cream cheese, Parmesan cheese, mozzarella cheese, green onions, roasted peppers, black pepper, red pepper and salt. Spread mixture in 2-quart baking dish sprayed with vegetable cooking spray.

Cover and bake at 400°F 20 minutes or until bubbly. Serve with pita or bagel chips for dipping.   *Makes 8 servings*

N U T R I T I O N A L   A N A L Y S I S

Per serving:

Calories	80	% Calories from fat	4%
Protein	9g	Sodium	565mg
Fat	.33g		

COCKTAIL STUFFED MUSHROOMS

30 to 40 medium-size mushrooms
1 (14-ounce) package Healthy Choice® Low Fat
    Polska Kielbasa
   Vegetable cooking spray
³⁄₄ cup minced onion
¹⁄₂ cup minced fresh parsley
 2 teaspoons minced garlic
¹⁄₂ teaspoon ground fennel
¹⁄₂ teaspoon salt (optional)
¹⁄₄ teaspoon black pepper
¹⁄₈ teaspoon crushed red pepper
1 can Healthy Choice® Recipe Creations™ Cream of
    Roasted Garlic Condensed Soup
¹⁄₃ cup fat free shredded Parmesan cheese

Wash mushrooms well. Remove stems and mince; set caps aside. In food processor, process Kielbasa until ground. In large nonstick skillet sprayed with vegetable cooking spray, sauté minced mushroom stems, Kielbasa, onion, parsley, garlic, fennel, salt, black pepper and red pepper. Cook until onion is tender.

Remove skillet from heat; add soup to meat mixture and blend well. Fill mushroom caps, dividing meat mixture evenly among caps. Sprinkle with Parmesan cheese. Bake at 400°F 20 to 22 minutes.

Makes 20 servings

NUTRITIONAL ANALYSIS

Per serving:

Calories	45	% Calories from fat	16%
Protein	4g	Sodium	310mg
Fat	1g		

CROWN OF SALMON APPETIZER

1 can **Healthy Choice® Recipe Creations™ Cream of**
   Celery with Sautéed Onion & Garlic
   Condensed Soup, divided
2 pounds **deboned and skinned halibut or other**
   firm white fish, cut into 1-inch cubes
¼ teaspoon **dried thyme leaves**
⅛ teaspoon **ground nutmeg**
   Vegetable cooking spray
6 ounces **smoked salmon (lox), thinly sliced**
¼ cup **nonfat milk**
1½ tablespoons **lemon juice**

In food processor, combine half the soup, fish, thyme and nutmeg. Process 30 seconds or until mixture resembles thick pudding. Generously spray 1-quart ring mold with vegetable cooking spray. Press salmon slices into bottom and side of mold. Carefully spoon mousse into ring mold without moving salmon slices. Gently bang mold on flat surface to remove any air bubbles.

Cover mold with wax paper sprayed with vegetable cooking spray; cover waxed paper with flat lid. Place ring mold in roasting pan. Pour hot water into pan to reach two-thirds up side of mold. Bake at 350°F 1 hour. Mousse is done when it is springy to the touch and shrinks from side of mold. Let stand 10 minutes to cool before unmolding.

In small saucepan, combine remaining soup, milk and lemon juice; mix well. Simmer until heated through. Unmold ring onto serving platter. Fill center of ring with favorite green vegetable or salad. Spoon sauce around outside of mousse ring. Serve with toasted bread rounds or crackers.   *Makes 12 servings*

NUTRITIONAL ANALYSIS

Per serving:

Calories	140	% Calories from fat	22%
Protein	22g	Sodium	480mg
Fat	3.5g		

Crown of Salmon Appetizer

Anytime Salads, Soups & Sandwiches

GARLIC CHICKEN CAESAR SALAD

DRESSING
- 1 can Healthy Choice® Recipe Creations™ Cream of Roasted Garlic Condensed Soup
- ½ cup fat free, low sodium chicken broth
- ¼ cup balsamic vinegar
- ¼ cup fat free shredded Parmesan cheese, divided
- 1 tablespoon low sodium Worcestershire sauce

SALAD
- 2 heads romaine lettuce, torn into 2-inch pieces
- 4 grilled boneless, skinless chicken breast halves, cut into 2-inch strips
- ½ cup fat free herb-seasoned croutons

In food processor or blender, combine soup, chicken broth, vinegar, 2 tablespoons Parmesan cheese and Worcestershire sauce; process until smooth. In large salad bowl, combine lettuce and 1 cup dressing; toss well to coat. Top with chicken and croutons; sprinkle with remaining 2 tablespoons cheese. *Makes 8 servings*

NUTRITIONAL ANALYSIS

Per serving:

Calories	130	% Calories from fat	15%
Protein	16g	Sodium	330mg
Fat	2g		

OPEN–FACED EGGPLANT MELT

**1 can Healthy Choice® Recipe Creations™ Tomato
    with Garden Herbs Condensed Soup
¼ cup fat free, low sodium chicken broth
3 sandwich-size English muffins, split and toasted
    Vegetable cooking spray
1 small eggplant, cut crosswise into 1-inch slices
    and grilled
½ cup roasted red bell pepper strips, drained
    (6 strips)
6 slices Healthy Choice® Low Fat Smoked Ham
½ cup Healthy Choice® Fat Free Shredded
    Mozzarella Cheese**

In small bowl, combine soup and chicken broth; mix well. Set aside. Place toasted muffin halves in single layer in shallow baking dish sprayed with vegetable cooking spray. Spread 1 tablespoon soup mixture on each muffin half. Top each muffin half with 1 slice eggplant, 1 bell pepper strip and 1 slice ham.

Pour remaining soup mixture evenly over sandwiches and sprinkle with cheese. Cover and bake at 350°F 10 minutes or until cheese is melted and sandwiches are heated through.   *Makes 6 servings*

NUTRITIONAL ANALYSIS

Per serving:

Calories	100	% Calories from fat	9%
Protein	7g	Sodium	360mg
Fat	1g		

ORIENTAL CHICKEN AND BROCCOLI SOUP

Vegetable cooking spray
1 cup sliced mushrooms
½ cup chopped onion
½ cup green or red bell pepper, cut into thin
    1½-inch strips
2 cloves garlic, minced
1 can Healthy Choice® Recipe Creations™ Cream of
    Roasted Chicken with Herbs Condensed Soup
1 (14½-ounce) can fat free, low sodium chicken
    broth
2 cups nonfat milk
½ teaspoon salt (optional)
⅛ teaspoon black pepper
½ cup uncooked rice
1 cup broccoli florets

In large saucepan sprayed with vegetable cooking spray, sauté mushrooms, onion, bell pepper and garlic until pepper is crisp-tender. Stir in soup and chicken broth until smooth. Add milk, salt and black pepper; bring to a boil, stirring occasionally.

Add rice to saucepan; cover and simmer 20 minutes over low heat. Add broccoli; cook 5 minutes or until broccoli is tender.

Makes 6 servings

NUTRITIONAL ANALYSIS

Per serving:

Calories	140	% Calories from fat	10%
Protein	7g	Sodium	330mg
Fat	1.5g		

BREAKFAST STRATA

1 can Healthy Choice® Recipe Creations™ Cream of
Mushroom with Cracked Pepper & Herbs
Condensed Soup
2 cups fat free egg substitute (equivalent to 8 eggs)
1 cup nonfat milk
¼ cup sliced green onions
1 teaspoon dry mustard
½ teaspoon salt (optional)
Vegetable cooking spray
6 slices reduced fat white bread, cut into 1-inch
cubes
4 links reduced fat precooked breakfast sausage,
thinly sliced

In medium bowl, combine soup, egg substitute, milk, green onions,
mustard and salt; mix well. In 2-quart baking dish sprayed with
vegetable cooking spray, combine bread cubes, sausage and soup
mixture; toss to coat. Bake at 350°F 30 to 35 minutes or until set.

Makes 6 servings

NUTRITIONAL ANALYSIS

Per serving:

Calories	110	% Calories from fat	20%
Protein	11g	Sodium	400mg
Fat	2.5g		

Breakfast Strata

CREAMY LITE CHICKEN SALAD

1 pound shredded cooked chicken *or* 2 (10-ounce)
    cans white chicken in water, drained
1 can Healthy Choice® Recipe Creations™ Cream of
    Roasted Chicken with Herbs Condensed Soup
½ cup sliced celery
¼ cup sliced green onions
2 tablespoons Dijon mustard
1½ teaspoons salt free ground herbs and spices
1 teaspoon *each* red wine vinegar and dried basil
    leaves

In medium bowl, combine chicken, soup, celery, green onions, mustard, herbs, vinegar and basil; mix well. Cover and refrigerate until ready to serve. *Makes 4 servings*

NUTRITIONAL ANALYSIS

Per serving:

Calories	240	% Calories from fat	23%
Protein	37g	Sodium	310mg
Fat	6g		

JAMESPORT SCALLOP CHOWDER

Vegetable cooking spray
1 cup sliced onion
½ cup diced red bell pepper
2 cloves garlic, minced
1 slice bacon, chopped
2 cups *each* fat free, low sodium chicken broth and
    diced, peeled potatoes
1 can Healthy Choice® Recipe Creations™ Cream of
    Celery with Sautéed Onion & Garlic
    Condensed Soup
10 ounces fresh bay scallops
¼ cup minced fresh parsley

In medium saucepan sprayed with vegetable cooking spray, sauté onion, pepper, garlic and bacon until onion is tender. Add chicken broth and potatoes; bring to a boil. Reduce heat; cover and simmer 15 minutes. Add soup; mix well. Stir in scallops. Simmer 3 to 4 minutes, stirring occasionally. Sprinkle with parsley. *Makes 6 servings*

NUTRITIONAL ANALYSIS

Per serving:

Calories	150	% Calories from fat	17%
Protein	12g	Sodium	450mg
Fat	3g		

PITA POCKETS

1 can Healthy Choice® Recipe Creations™ Tomato with Garden Herbs Condensed Soup
¼ cup fat free sour cream
Vegetable cooking spray
1 pound ground turkey
½ cup *each* Healthy Choice® Fat Free Shredded Cheddar Cheese and sliced green onions
½ teaspoon salt (optional)
3 pita bread rounds, cut in half to form pockets
1 cup *each* shredded lettuce and diced tomato

In small bowl, combine soup and sour cream; mix well. Set aside. In large nonstick skillet sprayed with vegetable cooking spray, cook turkey over medium-high heat until no longer pink; drain.

Add soup mixture, cheese, onions and salt to skillet; mix well. Reduce heat; cover and simmer 5 minutes or until cheese is melted. Fill pita bread pockets with turkey mixture. Garnish with lettuce and tomato. *Makes 6 servings*

NUTRITIONAL ANALYSIS

Per serving:

Calories	270	% Calories from fat	24%
Protein	21g	Sodium	430mg
Fat	7g		

GAZPACHO

2 cups Hunt's® Low Sodium Tomato Juice
1 (14½-ounce) can fat free, low sodium beef broth
1 can Healthy Choice® Recipe Creations™ Tomato
  with Garden Herbs Condensed Soup
1½ cups *each* peeled and diced cucumbers and diced
  green bell peppers
1¼ cups *each* shredded carrots and diced celery
½ cup sliced green onions
¼ cup chopped fresh parsley
2 cloves garlic, minced
1 tablespoon lime juice
2 teaspoons low sodium Worcestershire sauce
½ teaspoon salt (optional)
  Fat free sour cream
  Chopped cilantro

In large bowl, combine tomato juice, beef broth, soup, cucumbers, peppers, carrots, celery, green onions, parsley, garlic, lime juice, Worcestershire sauce and salt. Chill at least 2 hours to blend flavors. Top with desired amount of sour cream and cilantro.

Makes 4 to 6 servings

NUTRITIONAL ANALYSIS

Per serving:

Calories	80	% Calories from fat	6%
Protein	4g	Sodium	210mg
Fat	.5g		

Gazpacho

CREAM OF CARROT SOUP

1 pound carrots, peeled and cut into 1-inch pieces
½ cup water
1 can Healthy Choice® Recipe Creations™ Cream of
      Celery with Sautéed Onion & Garlic
      Condensed Soup
2 cups nonfat milk
1 tablespoon lemon juice
½ teaspoon *each* sugar, dried dill weed, garlic
      powder and onion powder
½ teaspoon salt (optional)
3 teaspoons sour cream (optional)

In medium saucepan, combine carrots and water; bring to a boil.
Reduce heat; cover and cook 20 to 25 minutes or until carrots are very
tender. In food processor or blender, process carrots and water until
puréed. Add soup, milk, lemon juice, sugar, dill, garlic powder, onion
powder and salt; process until well blended. Return mixture to
saucepan and cook over medium heat until heated through. Top each
serving with ½ teaspoon sour cream, if desired.   *Makes 6 servings*

NUTRITIONAL ANALYSIS

Per serving:

Calories	90	% Calories from fat	10%
Protein	4g	Sodium	240mg
Fat	1g		

SLIM JIM'S SLOPPY JOE

½ pound *each* lean ground beef and ground turkey
½ cup chopped onion
1 can Healthy Choice® Recipe Creations™ Tomato
      with Garden Herbs Condensed Soup
2 tablespoons Healthy Choice® Low Sodium
      Ketchup
1 tablespoon low sodium steak sauce
¾ cup water
8 light hamburger buns, toasted
      Lettuce leaves
      Sliced tomatoes

In large skillet, brown beef and turkey with onion; drain. Add soup, ketchup, steak sauce and water; blend well. Simmer over low heat 5 minutes or until heated through. Top each bun with lettuce leaf, tomato slice and ⅓ cup meat mixture. *Makes 8 sandwiches*

NUTRITIONAL ANALYSIS

Per serving:

Calories	200	% Calories from fat	28%
Protein	10g	Sodium	290mg
Fat	6g		

TUSCANY BEAN & PASTA SOUP

Vegetable cooking spray
½ cup chopped onion
2 cloves garlic, minced
1 can Healthy Choice® Recipe Creations™ Cream of Mushroom with Cracked Pepper & Herbs Condensed Soup
2½ cups nonfat milk
1 (15-ounce) can cannellini beans, drained and rinsed
1 cup cooked small macaroni (shells or elbow)
2 teaspoons chopped fresh parsley
½ teaspoon chili powder
½ teaspoon salt (optional)
Crumbled cooked bacon for garnish (optional)

In medium saucepan sprayed with vegetable cooking spray, sauté onion and garlic until tender. Add soup, milk, beans, macaroni, parsley, chili powder and salt; mix well. Simmer 10 minutes, stirring occasionally. Garnish with bacon, if desired. *Makes 6 servings*

NUTRITIONAL ANALYSIS

Per serving:

Calories	150	% Calories from fat	5%
Protein	8g	Sodium	410mg
Fat	1g		

TURKEY & CHEESE STUFFED POTATOES

6 baking potatoes, washed and pierced
2 cups frozen vegetables (such as broccoli, cauliflower, zucchini, carrots), thawed and drained
1½ cups ½-inch reduced fat cooked turkey breast cubes
1 can Healthy Choice® Recipe Creations™ Cream of Broccoli with Cheddar and Onion Condensed Soup
½ cup *each* reduced fat sour cream and nonfat milk
¼ teaspoon *each* garlic powder and pepper
½ cup sliced green onions

Bake or microwave potatoes to desired doneness. In medium saucepan, combine vegetables, turkey, soup, sour cream, milk, garlic powder and pepper; mix well. Simmer 5 minutes, stirring occasionally.

Cut warm potatoes lengthwise and squeeze potatoes to open. Spoon equal portions of soup mixture down centers of potatoes. Sprinkle with green onions.   *Makes 6 servings*

NUTRITIONAL ANALYSIS

Per serving:

Calories	210	% Calories from fat	17%
Protein	17g	Sodium	240mg
Fat	4g		

Turkey & Cheese Stuffed Potato

HEALTHY® CHOICE
CONDENSED SOUP
RECIPE CREATIONS™

Tantalizing Pastas

SAUSAGE AND BOW TIE BASH

1 can Healthy Choice® Recipe Creations™ Tomato
with Garden Herbs Condensed Soup
¼ cup nonfat milk
Vegetable cooking spray
½ cup *each* diced onion and green bell pepper
2 cloves garlic, minced
½ cup sliced mushrooms
½ teaspoon salt (optional)
1 (7-ounce package) Healthy Choice® Low Fat
Smoked Sausage, cut into ⅛-inch slices
4 cups cooked bow tie pasta

In small bowl, combine soup and milk; mix well. Set aside. In large nonstick skillet sprayed with vegetable cooking spray, sauté onion, pepper and garlic until tender. Add mushrooms and salt; cook 2 to 3 minutes. Add sausage and soup mixture; mix well. Reduce heat; cover and simmer 2 minutes longer. Add pasta and toss until coated with sauce. *Makes 6 servings*

NUTRITIONAL ANALYSIS

Per serving:

Calories	440	% Calories from fat	6%
Protein	22g	Sodium	410mg
Fat	3g		

PENNE PASTA SALAD

6 cups cooked penne pasta
2 cups shredded cooked skinless chicken breast
1 cup chopped red onion
¾ cup *each* chopped red or green bell pepper and
    sliced zucchini
1 (4-ounce) can sliced black olives, drained
1 teaspoon crushed red pepper
1 teaspoon salt (optional)
1 Healthy Choice® Recipe Creations™ Cream of
    Roasted Chicken with Herbs Condensed Soup
½ cup *each* lemon juice and fat free shredded
    Parmesan cheese
½ cup shredded fresh basil (optional)

In large bowl, combine pasta, chicken, onion, bell pepper, zucchini, olives, red pepper and salt; toss lightly. In small bowl, combine soup and lemon juice; mix well. Pour soup mixture over pasta salad; mix well. Sprinkle with Parmesan cheese and basil, if desired.

Makes 8 servings

N U T R I T I O N A L   A N A L Y S I S

Per serving:

Calories	258	% Calories from fat	22%
Protein	21g	Sodium	380mg
Fat	6g		

Penne Pasta Salad

CAPONATA PASTA TOPPER

**1 can Healthy Choice® Recipe Creations™ Tomato
with Garden Herbs Condensed Soup
¼ cup water
Vegetable cooking spray
1 small eggplant, diced (about 3 cups)
½ cup diced onion
2 cloves garlic, minced
4 cups hot cooked pasta**

In small bowl, combine soup and water; set aside. In large skillet sprayed with vegetable cooking spray, sauté eggplant, onion and garlic over medium-high heat until tender. Add soup mixture. Reduce heat; cover and simmer 10 minutes or until heated through. Serve over hot pasta.   *Makes 4 servings*

NUTRITIONAL ANALYSIS

Per serving:

Calories	270	% Calories from fat	6%
Protein	9g	Sodium	180mg
Fat	1.5g		

CHICKEN TETRAZZINI

**Vegetable cooking spray
2 cups sliced mushrooms
½ cup chopped onion
1 can Healthy Choice® Recipe Creations™ Cream of
Roasted Chicken with Herbs Condensed Soup
½ cup nonfat milk
1½ tablespoons dry sherry
½ teaspoon salt (optional)
2 cups 1-inch cooked chicken cubes
⅓ cup fat free shredded Parmesan cheese, divided
¼ cup chopped fresh parsley
4 cups cooked spaghetti**

In large saucepan sprayed with vegetable cooking spray, sauté mushrooms and onion until tender. Stir in soup, milk, sherry and salt;

heat through. Add chicken, ¼ cup Parmesan cheese and parsley; blend well. Add cooked spaghetti; toss to coat. Top with remaining Parmesan cheese. *Makes 4 servings*

N U T R I T I O N A L   A N A L Y S I S
Per serving:

Calories	390	% Calories from fat	16%
Protein	27g	Sodium	410mg
Fat	7g		

CREAMY CHICKEN AND SPINACH PASTA

1 can Healthy Choice® Recipe Creations™ Cream of
   Roasted Chicken with Herbs Condensed Soup
1 (3-ounce) package fat free cream cheese,
   softened
1 cup fat free, low sodium chicken broth
¼ cup fat free shredded Parmesan cheese
½ teaspoon salt (optional)
   Dash hot pepper sauce
1 (10-ounce) package frozen chopped spinach,
   thawed and drained
1 tablespoon lemon juice
1 (16-ounce) box fusilli pasta, cooked

In medium microwavable bowl, combine soup, cream cheese, chicken broth, Parmesan cheese, salt and hot pepper sauce. Cover and microwave on HIGH 2 to 3 minutes; whisk until smooth and blended. Add spinach and lemon juice. Microwave on HIGH 2 to 3 minutes or until hot, stirring after 1 minute. Combine pasta and soup mixture in large bowl, stirring until well coated. *Makes 4 to 6 servings*

N U T R I T I O N A L   A N A L Y S I S
Per serving:

Calories	330	% Calories from fat	7%
Protein	15g	Sodium	400mg
Fat	2.5g		

LASAGNA ROLL-UPS

Vegetable cooking spray
1 pound ground turkey breast or extra-lean ground
   beef
½ cup chopped onion
2 cloves garlic, minced
1 can Healthy Choice® Recipe Creations™ Tomato
   with Garden Herbs Condensed Soup
1 cup chopped zucchini
¾ cup water
1 (15-ounce) container fat free ricotta cheese
½ cup Healthy Choice® Fat Free Shredded
   Mozzarella Cheese
1 egg
4 cooked lasagna noodles

In large nonstick skillet sprayed with vegetable cooking spray, cook turkey, onion and garlic until turkey is no longer pink and onion is tender. Add soup, zucchini and water; simmer 5 minutes. Pour soup mixture into shallow 2-quart baking dish.

In medium bowl, combine ricotta and mozzarella cheeses and egg; mix well. Lay lasagna noodles on flat surface; spread ½ cup cheese mixture on each noodle. Roll up noodles, enclosing filling; place rolls seam sides down over soup mixture.

Cover and bake at 375°F 30 minutes; uncover and continue baking 10 minutes longer or until sauce is bubbly. Place lasagna rolls on serving dish; spoon remaining sauce over rolls.   *Makes 4 servings*

N U T R I T I O N A L   A N A L Y S I S

Per serving:

Calories	404	% Calories from fat	14%
Protein	52g	Sodium	558mg
Fat	6g		

Lasagna Roll-Ups

BISTRO PASTA SPINACH SALAD

DRESSING
- ½ cup *each* sun-dried tomatoes, boiling water and no-salt-added tomato juice
- 1 can Healthy Choice® Recipe Creations™ Tomato with Garden Herbs Condensed Soup
- ¼ cup red wine vinegar
- 1 tablespoon olive oil
- 1 clove garlic
- ½ teaspoon salt (optional)
- ⅛ teaspoon pepper

SALAD
- 4 cups *each* cooked small pasta shells and spinach leaves, torn into bite-size pieces
- 1 cup sliced cucumbers
- 1 (4.5-ounce) jar marinated artichokes, drained and chopped
- ½ cup thinly sliced red onion
- 2 tablespoons sliced black olives
- 1 tablespoon fat free shredded Parmesan cheese

For dressing, in small bowl, cover sun-dried tomatoes with boiling water; let stand 20 minutes. In food processor, process tomatoes, water, tomato juice, soup, vinegar, oil, garlic, salt and pepper until smooth. In large bowl, combine pasta, spinach, cucumbers, artichokes, onion, olives and cheese. Pour 1 cup dressing over salad and toss well to coat. *Makes 6 servings*

Note: *Store remaining dressing in an airtight container in refrigerator up to 4 days.*

Serving suggestion: *Serve dressing over hot cooked pasta.*

NUTRITIONAL ANALYSIS

Per serving:			
Calories	219	% Calories from fat	23%
Protein	8g	Sodium	304mg
Fat	6g		

Bistro Pasta Spinach Salad

FETTUCCINE PASTA PRIMAVERA

**1 can Healthy Choice® Recipe Creations™ Cream of
  Roasted Garlic Condensed Soup**
⅓ cup nonfat milk
½ teaspoon Italian seasoning
½ teaspoon salt (optional)
**⅛ teaspoon fennel seeds, crushed
  Vegetable cooking spray**
**4 cups sliced fresh vegetables (peppers, zucchini,
  carrots, asparagus) or thawed frozen vegetables**
½ cup coarsely chopped fresh tomato
4 cups hot cooked fettuccine

In small bowl, mix soup, milk, Italian seasoning, salt and fennel; set aside. Spray large nonstick skillet with vegetable cooking spray. Sauté vegetables over medium heat 4 to 5 minutes.* Stir in soup mixture; simmer 3 to 4 minutes. Add tomato; mix well. Serve over hot fettuccine.

Makes 6 servings

*½ pound cooked chicken, turkey sausage or shrimp may be added at this point.

N U T R I T I O N A L   A N A L Y S I S

Per serving:

Calories	206	% Calories from fat	9%
Protein	10g	Sodium	208mg
Fat	1g		

Per serving (with ½ pound shredded chicken):

Calories	244	% Calories from fat	7%
Protein	17g	Sodium	226mg
Fat	2g		

Per serving (with ½ pound sliced turkey sausage):

Calories	267	% Calories from fat	17%
Protein	16g	Sodium	450mg
Fat	5g		

Per serving (with ½ pound shrimp):

Calories	231	% Calories from fat	6%
Protein	15g	Sodium	270mg
Fat	1g		

Fettuccine Pasta Primavera

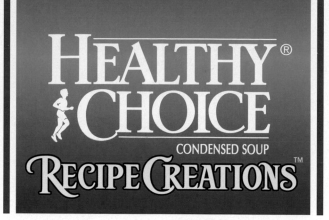

HEALTHY CHOICE®
CONDENSED SOUP
RECIPE CREATIONS™

Satisfying Vegetarian Entrées & Sides

ZUCCHINI MEDLEY

1 can Healthy Choice® Recipe Creations™ Tomato
    with Garden Herbs Condensed Soup
1 tablespoon lemon juice
1 teaspoon sugar
½ teaspoon garlic powder
½ teaspoon salt (optional)
6 cups ½-inch diagonal zucchini slices
1 cup *each* thinly sliced onion and coarsely
    chopped green bell pepper
½ cup sliced mushrooms
2 tablespoon fat free shredded Parmesan cheese

In large saucepan, combine soup, lemon juice, sugar, garlic powder and salt; mix well. Add zucchini, onion, pepper and mushrooms; mix well. Bring to a boil; reduce heat. Cover and cook 20 to 25 minutes or until vegetables are crisp-tender, stirring occasionally. Sprinkle with cheese before serving. *Makes 6 servings*

NUTRITIONAL ANALYSIS

Per serving:

Calories	80	% Calories from fat	7%
Protein	3g	Sodium	160mg
Fat	.5g		

POTATO AND VEGETABLE BAKE

2½ pounds new red potatoes, diced
1 (16-ounce) bag frozen broccoli and vegetable
    medley
1 can Healthy Choice® Recipe Creations™ Cream of
    Broccoli with Cheddar and Onion Condensed
    Soup
½ cup fat free sour cream
½ teaspoon salt (optional)
⅛ teaspoon black pepper
    Vegetable cooking spray
¼ cup fat free shredded Parmesan cheese
2 tablespoons chopped fresh chives

In large bowl, combine potatoes, vegetable medley, soup, sour cream, salt and pepper; mix well. Place mixture in 4-quart baking dish sprayed with vegetable cooking spray. Sprinkle with cheese and chives. Cover and bake at 400°F 1 hour or until potatoes are tender.

Makes 8 servings

NUTRITIONAL ANALYSIS

Per serving:

Calories	159	% Calories from fat	5%
Protein	6g	Sodium	233mg
Fat	1g		

CREAMED CABBAGE

8 cups coarsely chopped cabbage
1 tablespoon low fat margarine
1 can Healthy Choice® Recipe Creations™ Cream of
    Celery with Sautéed Onions & Garlic
    Condensed Soup
1 cup nonfat milk
½ teaspoon ground nutmeg
½ teaspoon salt (optional)

In large saucepan, sauté cabbage in hot margarine 2 to 3 minutes. Reduce heat; cover and cook 8 minutes, stirring often.

In small bowl, combine soup, milk, nutmeg and salt; mix well. Add soup mixture to cabbage; mix well. Cook 3 to 4 minutes or until heated through. *Makes 6 servings*

NUTRITIONAL ANALYSIS

Per serving:

Calories	80	% Calories from fat	25%
Protein	3g	Sodium	200mg
Fat	2.5g		

ULTIMATE GREEN BEAN CASSEROLE

1 can Healthy Choice® Recipe Creations™ Cream of Mushroom with Cracked Pepper & Herbs Condensed Soup
1 (16-ounce) bag frozen French-style green beans, thawed and drained
1 (8-ounce) can sliced water chestnuts, drained
1 cup thin 2-inch red bell pepper strips
  Vegetable cooking spray
2 tablespoons fat free shredded Parmesan cheese
1/3 cup chow mein noodles

In large bowl, combine soup, green beans, water chestnuts and pepper; mix well. Place mixture in 2-quart baking dish sprayed with vegetable cooking spray.

Cover and bake at 350°F 25 minutes. Sprinkle casserole with cheese; bake, uncovered, 5 minutes or until hot and bubbly. Sprinkle with noodles before serving. *Makes 6 servings*

NUTRITIONAL ANALYSIS

Per serving:

Calories	80	% Calories from fat	6%
Protein	3g	Sodium	260mg
Fat	.5g		

VEGETARIAN BROCCOLI CASSEROLE

Vegetable cooking spray
½ cup *each* chopped onion and celery
⅓ cup chopped red bell pepper
1 can Healthy Choice® Recipe Creations™ Cream of
    Broccoli with Cheddar and Onion Condensed
    Soup
¼ cup fat free sour cream
1 (10-ounce) package frozen chopped broccoli,
    thawed and drained
2 cups cooked rice
1 tomato, cut into ¼-inch slices

In large skillet sprayed with vegetable cooking spray, sauté onion, celery and pepper until crisp-tender. Stir in soup and sour cream. In 1½-quart baking dish sprayed with vegetable cooking spray, layer broccoli and rice. Top rice with soup mixture, spreading evenly.

Cover and bake at 350°F 20 minutes. Top with tomato slices; bake, uncovered, 10 minutes.   *Makes 6 servings*

NUTRITIONAL ANALYSIS

Per serving:

Calories	170	% Calories from fat	8%
Protein	6g	Sodium	230mg
Fat	1.5g		

Vegetarian Broccoli Casserole

VEGETABLE QUICHE

Vegetable cooking spray
2 cups frozen diced potatoes with onions and peppers, thawed
1 can Healthy Choice® Recipe Creations™ Cream of Mushroom with Cracked Pepper & Herbs Condensed Soup, divided
1 (16-ounce) package frozen mixed vegetables (such as zucchini, carrots and beans), thawed and drained
1 cup fat free egg substitute (equivalent to 4 eggs)
½ cup fat free shredded Parmesan cheese, divided
¼ cup nonfat milk
¼ teaspoon dried dill weed

In 9-inch pie plate sprayed with vegetable cooking spray, press potatoes onto bottom and side to form crust. Spray potatoes lightly with vegetable cooking spray. Bake at 400°F 15 minutes.

In small bowl, combine half the soup, mixed vegetables, egg substitute and half the cheese; mix well. Pour egg mixture into potato shell; sprinkle with remaining cheese. Bake at 375°F 35 to 40 minutes or until set.

In small saucepan, combine remaining soup, milk and dill; mix well. Simmer 5 minutes until heated through. Serve sauce with quiche.

Makes 6 servings

N U T R I T I O N A L   A N A L Y S I S

Per serving:

Calories	113	% Calories from fat	3%
Protein	9g	Sodium	436mg
Fat	1g		

Vegetable Quiche

BROCCOLI & CHEESE RICE PILAF

Vegetable cooking spray
¼ cup *each* minced onion and diced red bell pepper
2 cups raw precooked long grain rice
1⅓ cups water
1 can Healthy Choice® Recipe Creations™ Cream of Broccoli with Cheddar and Onion Condensed Soup
1 tablespoon minced fresh parsley
½ teaspoon salt (optional)

In medium saucepan sprayed with vegetable cooking spray, sauté onion and pepper until tender. Stir in rice. Add water, soup, parsley and salt; mix well. Bring to a boil; reduce heat. Cover and cook 10 minutes or until liquid is absorbed and rice is tender.

Makes 6 servings

N U T R I T I O N A L   A N A L Y S I S

Per serving:

Calories	170	% Calories from fat	6%
Protein	4g	Sodium	200mg
Fat	1g		

VEGETABLE MANICOTTI

**1 can Healthy Choice® Recipe Creations™ Cream of
Celery with Sautéed Onion & Garlic
Condensed Soup
¼ cup nonfat milk
2 tablespoons fat free shredded Parmesan cheese
½ teaspoon dried dill weed
3 medium zucchini, shredded (about 4 cups)
1 cup finely chopped red bell pepper
½ cup sliced green onions
½ teaspoon salt (optional)
⅛ teaspoon black pepper
¾ cup fat free ricotta cheese
Vegetable cooking spray
10 cooked manicotti shells**

In medium bowl, combine soup, milk, Parmesan cheese and dill; mix well. Set aside. In another medium bowl, combine zucchini, bell pepper, green onions, salt, black pepper and ricotta cheese; blend well.

In 13×9-inch baking dish sprayed with vegetable cooking spray, spread half the soup mixture. Fill manicotti shells with vegetable mixture; place filled shells over soup mixture. Pour remaining soup mixture over manicotti. Cover and bake at 350°F 30 to 35 minutes or until hot and bubbly. *Makes 5 servings*

NUTRITIONAL ANALYSIS

Per serving:

Calories	256	% Calories from fat	8%
Protein	16g	Sodium	330mg
Fat	2g		

FESTIVE POTATO SALAD

**1 can Healthy Choice® Recipe Creations™ Cream of
Celery with Sautéed Onion & Garlic
Condensed Soup
½ cup plain nonfat yogurt
3 tablespoons *each* red wine vinegar and sweet
relish
1 tablespoon Dijon mustard
1 clove garlic, minced
½ teaspoon salt (optional)
¼ teaspoon black pepper
4 russet potatoes, peeled, cooked and cut into
1-inch cubes
¾ cup sliced green onions
½ cup *each* diced red bell pepper and thinly sliced
celery
3 hard-boiled egg whites, chopped
½ teaspoon dry mustard**

In small bowl, combine soup, yogurt, vinegar, relish, mustard, garlic, salt and black pepper. Using wire whisk, blend until smooth. Set aside.

In large bowl, combine potatoes, green onions, bell pepper, celery, egg whites and mustard. Add soup mixture and toss gently until well coated. Refrigerate at least 1 hour to blend flavors.

Makes 8 servings

NUTRITIONAL ANALYSIS

Per serving:

Calories	110	% Calories from fat	8%
Protein	4g	Sodium	240mg
Fat	1g		

CREAMY MACARONI & CHEESE

1 can Healthy Choice® Recipe Creations™ Cream of
    Celery with Sautéed Onion & Garlic
    Condensed Soup
2 cups Healthy Choice® Fat Free Shredded Cheddar
    Cheese
½ cup nonfat milk
2 teaspoons *each* minced onion and diced red or
    green bell pepper
2 teaspoons horseradish
½ teaspoon salt (optional)
4 cups cooked small elbow macaroni
    Vegetable cooking spray
3 slices fat free sharp Cheddar cheese

In large bowl, combine soup, shredded cheese, milk, onion, pepper, horseradish and salt; mix well. Add macaroni; mix well.

Place macaroni mixture in 2-quart baking dish sprayed with vegetable cooking spray. Top with cheese slices; cover and bake at 375°F 30 minutes or until hot and bubbly.   *Makes 6 servings*

NUTRITIONAL ANALYSIS

Per serving:

Calories	247	% Calories from fat	6%
Protein	20g	Sodium	587mg
Fat	2g		

Creamy Macaroni & Cheese

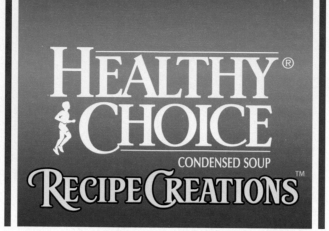

Healthy Poultry Entrées

HERB CHICKEN WITH APPLES

1 can Healthy Choice® Recipe Creations™ Cream of Roasted Chicken with Herbs Condensed Soup
½ cup nonfat milk
½ teaspoon Italian seasoning
Vegetable cooking spray
4 boneless, skinless chicken breast halves
2 medium red or green apples, cored and sliced
1 small onion, thinly sliced into rings

In small bowl, mix soup, milk and Italian seasoning; set aside. Heat large nonstick skillet sprayed with vegetable cooking spray over medium heat 1 minute. Add chicken; brown 5 minutes on each side. Remove from skillet.

Add apples and onion to skillet; cook until onion is tender. Stir in soup mixture. Return chicken to skillet; reduce heat to low. Cover and simmer 5 to 10 minutes or until chicken is no longer pink in center.

Makes 4 servings

NUTRITIONAL ANALYSIS

Per serving:

Calories	242	% Calories from fat	20%
Protein	29g	Sodium	297mg
Fat	5g		

WRAPPED GARLIC CHICKEN

4 boneless, skinless chicken breast halves
4 large sheets aluminum foil or parchment paper
½ teaspoon salt (optional)
1 cup sliced mushrooms
1 can Healthy Choice® Recipe Creations™ Cream of
**   Roasted Garlic Condensed Soup**
4 sprigs fresh rosemary *or* 1 teaspoon dried
**   rosemary leaves**

Place 1 chicken breast in center of each sheet of foil. Lightly season with salt. Top each breast with equal portions of mushrooms, soup and rosemary. Fold foil in half over chicken; seal all edges with double fold seals. Bake at 425°F 20 minutes or until chicken is no longer pink in center. *Makes 4 servings*

NUTRITIONAL ANALYSIS

Per serving:

Calories	186	% Calories from fat	19%
Protein	28g	Sodium	360mg
Fat	4g		

SKILLET CHICKEN WITH GARLIC & SUN-DRIED TOMATOES

Vegetable cooking spray
4 boneless, skinless chicken breast halves
1½ cups thinly sliced onions
½ cup finely chopped sun-dried tomatoes
1 can Healthy Choice® Recipe Creations™ Cream of
**   Roasted Garlic Condensed Soup**
¾ cup fat free, low sodium chicken broth
¼ cup white wine
½ teaspoon salt (optional)
¼ teaspoon pepper

In large skillet sprayed with vegetable cooking spray, cook chicken until brown on both sides. Arrange onions and tomatoes over chicken.

In small bowl, combine soup, chicken broth, wine, salt and pepper; mix well. Pour mixture over chicken. Cover and simmer 20 to 25 minutes or until chicken is no longer pink in center.

Makes 4 servings

NUTRITIONAL ANALYSIS

Per serving:

Calories	230	% Calories from fat	16%
Protein	29g	Sodium	450mg
Fat	4g		

LEMON CHICKEN WITH HERBS

1 can Healthy Choice® Recipe Creations™ Cream of Roasted Chicken with Herbs Condensed Soup
¼ cup nonfat milk
2 tablespoons lemon juice
2 tablespoons minced fresh parsley
Vegetable cooking spray
4 boneless, skinless chicken breast halves
½ cup sliced mushrooms
¼ cup chopped red onion

In small bowl, mix soup, milk, lemon juice and parsley; set aside. Heat large nonstick skillet sprayed with vegetable cooking spray over medium heat 1 minute. Add chicken; brown 5 minutes on each side. Remove from skillet. Add mushrooms and onion to skillet; sauté 2 to 3 minutes. Stir in soup mixture.

Return chicken to skillet; reduce heat to low. Cover and simmer 5 to 10 minutes or until chicken is no longer pink in center.

Makes 4 servings

NUTRITIONAL ANALYSIS

Per serving:

Calories	209	% Calories from fat	22%
Protein	29g	Sodium	290mg
Fat	5g		

SOUTHWESTERN TURKEY

1 can Healthy Choice® Recipe Creations™ Tomato
**   with Herbs Condensed Soup**
½ cup fat free sour cream
**   Vegetable cooking spray**
1 cup sliced green onions or yellow onion
½ cup *each* diced green chiles, frozen whole kernel
**   yellow corn and chopped red bell pepper**
2 cloves garlic, minced
1 pound turkey tenderloins, cut into thin 2-inch
**   strips**
½ teaspoon salt (optional)
**   Hot cooked rice (optional)**

In small bowl, combine soup and sour cream; mix well. Set aside. In large nonstick skillet sprayed with vegetable cooking spray, sauté onions, chiles, corn, pepper and garlic over medium-high heat until onions and pepper are tender.

Add turkey strips to skillet and brown evenly. Add soup mixture and salt, blending well; bring to a simmer. Reduce heat to low; cover and simmer 5 minutes. Serve with rice, if desired.   *Makes 4 servings*

NUTRITIONAL ANALYSIS

Per serving:

Calories	261	% Calories from fat	16%
Protein	28g	Sodium	301mg
Fat	5g		

Southwestern Turkey

ROSEMARY ORANGE CHICKEN

**1 can Healthy Choice® Recipe Creations™ Cream of
Celery with Sautéed Onion & Garlic
Condensed Soup
½ cup nonfat milk
1½ tablespoons orange marmalade
¼ teaspoon dried rosemary leaves
Vegetable cooking spray
4 boneless, skinless chicken breast halves
1 cup *each* julienne-cut carrots and zucchini**

In medium bowl, mix soup, milk, marmalade and rosemary; set aside. Heat large nonstick skillet sprayed with vegetable cooking spray over medium heat 1 minute. Add chicken; brown 5 minutes on each side. Remove from skillet.

Add carrots and zucchini to skillet; sauté 2 to 3 minutes. Stir in soup mixture. Return chicken to skillet. Reduce heat to low; cover and simmer 5 to 8 minutes or until chicken is no longer pink in center.   *Makes 4 servings*

NUTRITIONAL ANALYSIS

Per serving:

Calories	243	% Calories from fat	28%
Protein	29g	Sodium	350mg
Fat	5g		

Rosemary Orange Chicken

MEDITERRANEAN CHICKEN

1 can Healthy Choice® Recipe Creations™ Tomato
    with Garden Herbs Condensed Soup
½ cup water
¼ cup golden raisins
1 (2.25-ounce) can sliced black olives, drained
½ teaspoon *each* garlic powder and dried oregano
    leaves
    Vegetable cooking spray
4 boneless, skinless chicken breasts, cut into
    2×1-inch strips
1 cup sliced zucchini
½ cup thin red or green bell pepper strips
3 cups hot cooked rice

In medium bowl, mix soup, water, raisins, olives, garlic powder and oregano; set aside. In large nonstick skillet sprayed with vegetable cooking spray, sauté chicken over high heat until no longer pink in center. Remove from skillet.

Add zucchini and pepper to skillet; sauté 2 to 3 minutes. Reduce heat; stir in soup mixture. Return chicken to skillet and cook until heated through. Serve over rice.   *Makes 4 servings*

NUTRITIONAL ANALYSIS
Per serving:

Calories	434	% Calories from fat	9%
Protein	33g	Sodium	395mg
Fat	4g		

CHICKEN AND HAM ROLL–UPS

4 boneless, skinless chicken breast halves
1 can Healthy Choice® Recipe Creations™ Cream of
   Roasted Chicken with Herbs Condensed Soup,
   divided
½ teaspoon salt (optional)
4 slices Healthy Choice® Low Fat Deli Cooked Ham
1 egg white, slightly beaten
2 English muffins, finely crumbled
   Vegetable cooking spray
⅓ cup nonfat milk

Place chicken breasts between two sheets of plastic wrap. Pound firmly to ¼-inch thickness. Lay chicken breasts on work surface. Brush each with 1 tablespoon soup; season with salt. Place 1 slice of ham on each breast. Roll up each breast and secure with wooden picks. Brush with egg white and roll in English muffin crumbs. Place in shallow baking dish sprayed with vegetable cooking spray.

In small bowl, combine remaining soup and milk; mix well. Pour mixture around chicken breasts. Cover and bake at 350°F 30 minutes. Uncover and broil 5 inches from broiler flame until muffin crumbs are golden brown. Remove wooden picks before serving.

Makes 4 servings

NUTRITIONAL ANALYSIS

Per serving:

Calories	330	% Calories from fat	29%
Protein	36g	Sodium	520mg
Fat	10g		

HEALTHY CHOICE® TANGY OVEN–FRIED BBQ CHICKEN

1 cup all-purpose flour
1 tablespoon *each* garlic powder, onion powder
**   and poultry seasoning**
6 boneless, skinless chicken breast halves
½ teaspoon salt (optional)
**   Vegetable cooking spray**
1 can Healthy Choice® Recipe Creations™ Tomato
**   with Garden Herbs Condensed Soup**
¼ cup *each* low sodium Worcestershire sauce and
**   packed brown sugar**
2 tablespoons cider vinegar
½ cup chopped onion

In large bowl, combine flour, garlic powder, onion powder and poultry seasoning. Season chicken with salt. Coat chicken pieces with flour mixture and place on foil-lined baking sheet sprayed with vegetable cooking spray. Bake chicken at 350°F 20 minutes.

Meanwhile, in small saucepan, combine soup, Worcestershire sauce, brown sugar, vinegar and onion; bring to a boil over medium heat. Reduce heat to low; simmer 10 minutes. Baste chicken generously with 1 cup sauce, reserving remaining sauce. Continue baking 20 minutes or until no longer pink in center. Serve with remaining sauce for dipping.

Makes 4 to 6 servings

NUTRITIONAL ANALYSIS

Per serving:

Calories	310	% Calories from fat	11%
Protein	30g	Sodium	230mg
Fat	4g		

EASY CHICKEN À LA KING

**3 cooked boneless, skinless chicken breast halves,
shredded into bite-size pieces
1 can Healthy Choice® Recipe Creations™ Cream of
Celery with Sautéed Onion & Garlic
Condensed Soup
½ cup *each* sliced green onions and sliced
mushrooms
2 tablespoons nonfat milk
½ teaspoon salt (optional)
Vegetable cooking spray
2 English muffins, halved**

In medium bowl, combine chicken, soup, green onions, mushrooms, milk and salt; mix well. In four 6-ounce custard cups sprayed with vegetable cooking spray, place equal portions of chicken mixture. Top with English muffin halves, split sides down.

Place cups on cookie sheet; bake at 450°F 13 to 15 minutes or until muffins are golden brown and chicken mixture is hot and bubbly. Invert cups onto serving dish.   *Makes 4 servings*

N U T R I T I O N A L   A N A L Y S I S

Per serving:

Calories	230	% Calories from fat	17%
Protein	23g	Sodium	420mg
Fat	4g		

Easy Chicken à la King

GARLIC CHICKEN AND VEGETABLE SLAW

1 can Healthy Choice® Recipe Creations™ Cream of
    Roasted Garlic Condensed Soup
⅓ cup red wine vinegar
¼ cup plain nonfat yogurt
½ teaspoon sugar
½ teaspoon salt (optional)
¼ teaspoon pepper
5 cups shredded green cabbage
1 cup shredded red cabbage
1½ cups chopped, cooked chicken breast
½ cup *each* seeded, chopped tomato and shredded
    carrot
½ cup *each* sliced green onions and peeled,
    chopped cucumber

In food processor, combine soup, vinegar, yogurt, sugar, salt and pepper; process until smooth. Set aside.

In large bowl, combine green cabbage, red cabbage, chicken, tomato, carrot, green onions and cucumber. Add soup mixture and toss well to coat. Refrigerate at least 2 hours to blend flavors.

Makes 6 servings

NUTRITIONAL ANALYSIS

Per serving:

Calories	93	% Calories from fat	15%
Protein	11g	Sodium	238mg
Fat	2g		

Garlic Chicken and Vegetable Slaw

SPICY PEANUT CHICKEN

Vegetable cooking spray
4 boneless, skinless chicken breast halves, cut in
    half lengthwise
1 can Healthy Choice® Recipe Creations™ Cream of
    Roasted Chicken with Herbs Condensed Soup
2 tablespoons reduced fat peanut butter
½ cup *each* nonfat milk and ½-inch diagonal green
    onion slices
1 teaspoon chili powder
¼ teaspoon crushed red pepper

In large skillet sprayed with vegetable cooking spray, brown chicken on both sides. Remove chicken from skillet. Add soup, peanut butter, milk, green onions, chili powder and red pepper; blend well. Bring to a boil; return chicken to skillet. Cover and simmer over low heat 5 minutes or until chicken is no longer pink in center.

Makes 4 servings

NUTRITIONAL ANALYSIS

Per serving:

Calories	250	% Calories from fat	29%
Protein	31g	Sodium	340mg
Fat	8g		

CHICKEN DIABLO

1 can Healthy Choice® Recipe Creations™ Cream of
    Roasted Garlic Condensed Soup
¾ cup salsa
¼ teaspoon ground cumin
6 boneless, skinless chicken breast halves
1 (14-ounce) can quartered artichoke hearts,
    drained
1 (2.25-ounce) can sliced black olives, drained
2 tablespoons chopped fresh cilantro (optional)

In medium bowl, mix soup, salsa and cumin; set aside. Arrange chicken in 13×9-inch baking dish. Bake at 350°F 20 minutes. Place artichoke hearts around chicken. Top with soup mixture; sprinkle with black olives. Continue baking 25 to 30 minutes or until chicken is no longer pink in center. Sprinkle with cilantro before serving, if desired.

Makes 6 servings

NUTRITIONAL ANALYSIS

Per serving:

Calories	202	% Calories from fat	17%
Protein	30g	Sodium	563mg
Fat	4g		

CHICKEN DIVAN

- 1 can Healthy Choice® Recipe Creations™ Cream of Broccoli with Cheddar and Onion Condensed Soup
- ¼ cup nonfat milk
- ½ teaspoon salt (optional)
  Vegetable cooking spray
- 4 slices reduced fat white bread, toasted
- 4 boneless, skinless chicken breast halves, cooked
- 1 (10-ounce) box frozen broccoli spears, thawed and drained
- 2 tablespoons fat free shredded Parmesan cheese

In medium bowl, combine soup, milk and salt; mix well. In 1½-quart baking dish sprayed with vegetable cooking spray, place toast slices; top each slice with chicken breast half. Arrange broccoli spears over chicken. Pour soup mixture evenly over broccoli and sprinkle with Parmesan cheese. Cover and bake at 350°F 15 minutes or until hot and bubbly.

Makes 4 servings

NUTRITIONAL ANALYSIS

Per serving:

Calories	270	% Calories from fat	17%
Protein	34g	Sodium	530mg
Fat	5g		

FIESTA CHICKEN WITH GARLIC SOUR CREAM SAUCE

1 can Healthy Choice® Recipe Creations™ Cream of
    Roasted Garlic Condensed Soup
½ cup reduced fat sour cream
2 teaspoons lime juice
½ teaspoon ground cumin
    Vegetable cooking spray
3 boneless, skinless chicken breast halves, cut into
    1-inch cubes
2 cups frozen vegetables (corn, broccoli and red
    bell pepper), thawed and drained
½ cup Healthy Choice® Fat Free Shredded Cheddar
    Cheese
    Hot cooked rice (optional)

In small bowl, mix soup, sour cream, lime juice and cumin; set aside. Heat large nonstick skillet sprayed with vegetable cooking spray over medium-high heat 1 minute. Add chicken; sauté 4 to 5 minutes until chicken is no longer pink in center. Add vegetables and sauté 1 to 2 minutes.

Stir soup mixture into skillet; simmer over low heat 5 minutes. Sprinkle with cheese; serve over rice, if desired. *Makes 6 servings*

NUTRITIONAL ANALYSIS

Per serving:

Calories	242	% Calories from fat	17%
Protein	20g	Sodium	312mg
Fat	5g		

Fiesta Chicken with Garlic Sour Cream Sauce

Lean Meat
& Seafood Entrées

BAY VILLAGE SHRIMP

1 can Healthy Choice® Recipe Creations™ Cream of
  Celery with Sautéed Onion & Garlic
  Condensed Soup
1 pound fresh or thawed frozen shrimp, shelled and
  deveined
½ cup asparagus (fresh or thawed frozen), cut
  diagonally into 1-inch pieces
½ cup sliced mushrooms
¼ cup *each* sliced green onions and diced red bell
  pepper
½ teaspoon dried thyme
½ teaspoon salt (optional)
  Vegetable cooking spray
  Hot cooked rice (optional)

In large bowl, combine soup, shrimp, asparagus, mushrooms, green
onions, pepper, thyme and salt; mix well. Place in 2-quart baking dish
sprayed with vegetable cooking spray. Cover and bake at 375°F 30
minutes. Serve over rice, if desired.   *Makes 4 servings*

NUTRITIONAL ANALYSIS

Per serving:

Calories	135	% Calories from fat	15%
Protein	19g	Sodium	433mg
Fat	2g		

LEAN MEAT & SEAFOOD ENTRÉES

MEATLOAF RING WITH GARLIC MASHED POTATOES

4 large red potatoes, cubed
1 pound extra-lean ground beef
1 can Healthy Choice® Recipe Creations™ Cream of
    Roasted Garlic Condensed Soup, divided
3 slices fresh reduced fat white bread, processed to
    form crumbs
½ cup fat free egg substitute (equivalent to 2 eggs)
½ cup *each* shredded carrots and shredded zucchini
¼ cup *each* minced red bell pepper and minced
    onion
2 tablespoons minced fresh parsley, divided
1 teaspoon Italian seasoning
    Vegetable cooking spray
⅓ cup fat free cream cheese
½ teaspoon salt (optional)

In medium saucepan, combine potatoes and enough water to cover potatoes. Bring to a boil; cover and reduce heat to medium-high. Cook 20 to 25 minutes or until tender.

Meanwhile, combine beef, ⅓ cup soup, bread crumbs, egg substitute, carrots, zucchini, pepper, onion, 1 tablespoon parsley and Italian seasoning; mix well. In shallow round 2-quart baking dish sprayed with vegetable cooking spray, form beef mixture into ring around outer edge of dish, leaving center open. Bake at 400°F 20 to 25 minutes.

Drain potatoes; mash with potato masher. Add remaining soup, cream cheese and salt; mash until well mixed. Remove meatloaf from oven; mound potatoes in center. Place under broiler 5 minutes or until lightly browned. Sprinkle with remaining 1 tablespoon parsley.

Makes 6 servings

NUTRITIONAL ANALYSIS

Per serving:

Calories	317	% Calories from fat	21%
Protein	9g	Sodium	452mg
Fat	6g		

Meatloaf Ring with Garlic Mashed Potatoes

CALIFORNIA CRÊPES

1 can Healthy Choice® Recipe Creations™ Cream of
   Broccoli with Cheddar and Onion Condensed
   Soup, divided
1 cup nonfat milk, divided
1 cup fat free egg substitute (equivalent to 4 eggs)
   Vegetable cooking spray
1 cup sliced mushrooms
½ cup frozen spinach, thawed and drained
10 ounces ground pork tenderloin
½ teaspoon salt (optional)

In small bowl, combine half the soup with ½ cup milk; mix well. Set aside. In another bowl, combine remaining ½ cup milk and egg substitute; whisk until blended. Pour egg substitute mixture, ¼ cup at a time, onto hot 10-inch skillet sprayed with vegetable cooking spray. Swirl egg mixture to thinly cover bottom of skillet. Cook 2 minutes or until underside of crêpe is lightly browned. Remove crêpe carefully with spatula to warm plate; cover with paper towel. Repeat procedure to make 6 crêpes.

In same skillet, sauté mushrooms and spinach until liquid from mushrooms has evaporated; transfer to medium bowl. Add pork to skillet. Cook pork over medium-high heat until no longer pink; drain. Add to mushrooms and spinach with remaining soup; mix well.

Spoon mixture evenly over 6 crêpes; roll up crêpes. Arrange crêpes, seam sides down, in shallow baking dish sprayed with vegetable cooking spray. Pour reserved soup mixture over crêpes; cover and bake at 350°F 30 minutes.   *Makes 6 servings*

NUTRITIONAL ANALYSIS

Per serving:

Calories	150	% Calories from fat	25%
Protein	18g	Sodium	330mg
Fat	4g		

SEAFOOD AND SHELLS

1 can Healthy Choice® Recipe Creations™ Cream of
    Celery with Sautéed Onion & Garlic
    Condensed Soup
½ cup nonfat milk
1 tablespoon olive oil
8 ounces halibut or other firm white fish, cut into
    1-inch pieces
1 (6-ounce) package frozen cooked crabmeat,
    thawed
2 medium zucchini, thinly sliced
1 leek, white part only, sliced
1 teaspoon dried thyme leaves
½ teaspoon *each* dried dill weed and garlic powder
½ teaspoon salt (optional)
8 cherry tomatoes, halved
4 cups hot cooked small pasta shells

In small bowl, combine soup and milk; mix well. Set aside. In large skillet, heat oil. Add fish, crabmeat, zucchini, leek, thyme, dill, garlic powder and salt; sauté 3 to 4 minutes or until fish flakes and zucchini is crisp-tender.

Add soup mixture to skillet. Heat until sauce is bubbly, stirring gently. Remove from heat. Add tomatoes; mix lightly. Serve over pasta.

Makes 6 servings

NUTRITIONAL ANALYSIS

Per serving:

Calories	254	% Calories from fat	18%
Protein	19g	Sodium	496mg
Fat	5g		

MONDAY NIGHT PORK AND BEANS

Vegetable cooking spray
½ cup *each* sliced onion and diced green bell
    pepper
2 cloves garlic, minced
1 can Healthy Choice® Recipe Creations™ Tomato
    with Garden Herbs Condensed Soup
1 (15-ounce) can white beans, rinsed and drained
10 ounces pork tenderloin, trimmed and cubed
½ cup firmly packed brown sugar
½ teaspoon salt (optional)

In large saucepan sprayed with vegetable cooking spray, sauté onion, pepper and garlic until tender. Add soup, beans, pork, brown sugar and salt; cover and simmer 1 hour.   *Makes 6 servings*

NUTRITIONAL ANALYSIS

Per serving:

Calories	290	% Calories from fat	9%
Protein	21g	Sodium	160mg
Fat	3g		

BISTRO SALMON STEAKS

**1 can Healthy Choice® Recipe Creations™ Cream of
    Celery with Sautéed Onion & Garlic
    Condensed Soup**
½ cup nonfat milk
2 teaspoons Dijon mustard
½ teaspoon dried dill weed
1 cup seedless red grapes, halved, divided
**4 (6- to 8-ounce) boneless salmon steaks or fillets,
    ¾ inch thick***
1 tablespoon chopped fresh parsley

In small bowl, combine soup, milk, mustard and dill; mix well. In 13×9-inch baking dish, spread half the soup mixture and half the grapes. Place fish over soup mixture. Pour remaining soup mixture over fish and sprinkle with remaining grapes.

Bake at 350°F 20 to 25 minutes or until fish begins to flake when tested with fork. Sprinkle with parsley.   *Makes 4 servings*

Halibut, swordfish or tuna may be substituted for salmon.

N U T R I T I O N A L   A N A L Y S I S

Per serving:

Calories	290	% Calories from fat	25%
Protein	36g	Sodium	390mg
Fat	8g		

Bistro Salmon Steak

FESTIVE STUFFED PEPPERS

1 can Healthy Choice® Recipe Creations™ Tomato
   with Garden Herbs Condensed Soup, divided
¼ cup water
8 ounces extra-lean ground beef or turkey
1 cup cooked rice
½ cup frozen corn, thawed
¼ cup *each* sliced celery and chopped red bell
   pepper
½ teaspoon Italian seasoning
2 green, yellow or red bell peppers, cut in half
   lengthwise, seeds removed

In small bowl, mix ¼ cup soup and water. Pour into 8×8-inch baking dish; set aside. In large skillet, brown beef over medium-high heat; drain well. In large bowl, combine remaining soup with cooked beef, rice, corn, celery, chopped pepper and Italian seasoning; mix well.

Fill pepper halves equally with beef mixture. Place stuffed peppers on top of soup mixture in baking dish. Cover and bake at 350°F 35 to 40 minutes. Place peppers on serving dish and spoon remaining sauce from baking dish over peppers.   *Makes 4 servings*

N U T R I T I O N A L   A N A L Y S I S

Per serving:

Calories	260	% Calories from fat	29%
Protein	15g	Sodium	215mg
Fat	8g		

Festive Stuffed Peppers

BLANQUETTE DE VEAU (VEAL STEW)

**1 can Healthy Choice® Recipe Creations™ Cream of
   Celery with Sautéed Onion & Garlic
   Condensed Soup
1 pound veal, cut into 1-inch cubes
1 cup *each* 1-inch onion, carrot and celery pieces
1 cup sliced mushrooms
½ cup nonfat milk
½ teaspoon dried thyme leaves
½ teaspoon salt (optional)
   Vegetable cooking spray
   Hot cooked rice or pasta (optional)**

In large bowl, combine soup, veal, onion, carrots, celery, mushrooms, milk, thyme and salt; mix well. Place in 2-quart baking dish sprayed with vegetable cooking spray. Cover and bake at 350°F 1 hour. Serve over rice or pasta, if desired.   *Makes 4 servings*

N U T R I T I O N A L   A N A L Y S I S
Per serving:

Calories	233	% Calories from fat	18%
Protein	29g	Sodium	350mg
Fat	5g		

POACHED WHITE FISH PROVENÇAL

**   Vegetable cooking spray
4 (4-ounce) halibut fillets or other firm white fish
1 can Healthy Choice® Recipe Creations™ Cream of
   Celery with Sautéed Onion & Garlic
   Condensed Soup
⅓ cup Rhine wine
1 tablespoon *each* lemon juice and clam juice
2 tablespoons minced fresh chives
½ teaspoon salt (optional)
¼ teaspoon dried tarragon leaves
⅛ teaspoon *each* white pepper and ground nutmeg**

In large nonstick skillet sprayed with vegetable cooking spray, lightly brown fish on both sides. Remove fish from skillet. Add soup, wine, lemon juice and clam juice to skillet; mix well. Add chives, salt, tarragon, pepper and nutmeg; bring to a simmer over medium-low heat, stirring constantly.

Return fish to skillet; cover and simmer 3 to 5 minutes or until fish begins to flake when tested with fork.   *Makes 4 servings*

NUTRITIONAL ANALYSIS

Per serving:

Calories	190	% Calories from fat	21%
Protein	23g	Sodium	330mg
Fat	4g		

MEDITERRANEAN CHILI

1 can Healthy Choice® Recipe Creations™ Tomato
   with Garden Herbs Condensed Soup
¼ cup water
1 cup fat free refried beans
   Vegetable cooking spray
10 ounces extra-lean ground beef
1 small eggplant, diced
½ cup *each* diced onion and diced green bell
   pepper
2 cloves garlic, minced
½ teaspoon chili powder
½ teaspoon salt (optional)

In medium bowl, combine soup, water and beans; mix well. Set aside. In large saucepan sprayed with vegetable cooking spray, cook beef until no longer pink; drain and set aside.

In same saucepan, sauté eggplant, onion, pepper, garlic, chili powder and salt over medium-high heat until vegetables are tender. Add soup mixture and beef; mix well. Simmer until hot and bubbly.

Makes 4 servings

NUTRITIONAL ANALYSIS

Per serving:

Calories	220	% Calories from fat	29%
Protein	6g	Sodium	470mg
Fat	6g		

BEEF AND CARAMELIZED ONIONS

1 can Healthy Choice® Recipe Creations™ Cream of
    Mushroom with Cracked Pepper & Herbs
    Condensed Soup
¾ cup nonfat milk
½ cup fat free sour cream
½ teaspoon salt (optional)
1 (14-ounce) can pearl onions, drained or 2 cups
    thinly sliced onions
1 clove garlic, minced
1 tablespoon low fat margarine
1 teaspoon sugar
1 tablespoon vinegar
1 cup sliced mushrooms
12 ounces sirloin steak, cut into 2×¼-inch slices
4 cups hot cooked yolk free egg noodles
1 tablespoon minced fresh parsley

In small bowl, mix soup, milk, sour cream and salt; set aside. In nonstick skillet, sauté onions and garlic in hot margarine over medium heat until lightly brown. Add sugar; cook until golden, stirring constantly. Stir in vinegar; cook 1 minute. Remove from skillet; set aside.

Add mushrooms to skillet; sauté mushrooms until lightly brown. Remove from skillet; set aside. Add steak; sauté over high heat until browned on both sides. Remove from skillet; drain skillet. Add soup mixture to skillet; cook over low heat until heated through. Return onions, mushrooms and steak to skillet. Heat 2 minutes. *(Do not boil.)* Serve over hot cooked noodles; garnish with parsley.

Makes 6 servings

NUTRITIONAL ANALYSIS

Per serving:

Calories	305	% Calories from fat	16%
Protein	21g	Sodium	495mg
Fat	5g		

Beef and Caramelized Onions

SHANGHAI BEEF

**1 can Healthy Choice® Recipe Creations™ Cream of
  Mushroom with Cracked Pepper & Herbs
  Condensed Soup**
⅓ cup nonfat milk
1½ teaspoons teriyaki sauce
¼ teaspoon garlic powder
⅛ teaspoon crushed red pepper (optional)
  Vegetable cooking spray
12 ounces sirloin steak,* cut into 2×¼-inch slices
¾ cup julienne-cut carrots
1 (8-ounce) can sliced water chestnuts, drained
**3 dried shiitake mushrooms, soaked, drained and
    sliced *or* 1 (4-ounce) can sliced mushrooms,
    drained**

In medium bowl, mix soup, milk, teriyaki sauce, garlic powder and red pepper; set aside. Heat large nonstick skillet sprayed with vegetable cooking spray over medium-high heat 1 minute. Add steak; sauté until brown on both sides. Remove from skillet.

Add carrots, water chestnuts and mushrooms to skillet; sauté 2 to 3 minutes. Stir in soup mixture; reduce heat and cook until heated through. Return steak to skillet; heat 1 minute.   *Makes 4 servings*

*Pork or chicken may be substituted for steak.

N U T R I T I O N A L   A N A L Y S I S

Per serving:

Calories	226	% Calories from fat	23%
Protein	22g	Sodium	490mg
Fat	6g		